Muriel Spark

by KARL MALKOFF

 *Columbia University Press*
NEW YORK & LONDON 1968

COLUMBIA ESSAYS ON MODERN WRITERS is a series of critical studies of English, Continental, and other writers whose works are of contemporary artistic and intellectual significance.

Editor: William York Tindall

Advisory Editors

Jacques Barzun   W. T. H. Jackson   Joseph A. Mazzeo   Justin O'Brien

Muriel Spark is Number 36 of the series

KARL MALKOFF is Assistant Professor of English at the City College of New York and is the author of *Theodore Roethke: An Introduction to the Poetry.*

Acknowledgment is made to the following for permission to quote from Muriel Spark's works: Harold Ober Associates; Macmillan and Co., Ltd.; Alfred A. Knopf, for selections from *The Girls of Slender Means* and *The Mandelbaum Gate*; and J. B. Lippincott Company, for selections from *The Comforters* (copyright © 1957 by Muriel Spark), *Robinson* (copyright © 1958 by Muriel Spark), *The Go-Away Bird* (copyright © 1958 by Muriel Spark), *Memento Mori* (copyright © 1959 by Muriel Spark), *The Ballad of Peckham Rye* (copyright © 1960 by Muriel Spark), *The Bachelors* (copyright © 1960 by Muriel Spark), and *The Prime of Miss Jean Brodie* (copyright © 1961 by Muriel Spark).

Muriel Spark

The Transfiguration of the Commonplace. That is the title of pig-eyed Sister Helena's famous treatise in *The Prime of Miss Jean Brodie;* it is also an appropriate description of the fictive method of Muriel Spark.

Approaching the novel with all the suspicions of a poet accosting an alien, and perhaps inferior, medium, Miss Spark uses a dazzling assortment of techniques to accomplish in prose what she had first attempted in verse: to create by cutting through the barriers of overused language and situation a sense of reality true to experience, an imaginative extension of the world, a lie that shows us things as they are—a supreme fiction.

But although it admits of endless variation, her apparently complex method is simple. She uses a momentous, sometimes supernatural event violently to shift perspective and reveal the bizarre underpinnings of the superficially conventional. The agent of transfiguration differs from novel to novel: a character's involvement in the process of writing the novel of which she is part; an airplane crash on a lonely island; a series of phone calls reminding the elderly recipients that they soon must die; a diabolical intruder descending upon a working-class community; the trial of a medium for fraudulent conversion; the betrayal of a charismatic schoolteacher by her most trusted disciple; a catastrophic fire at a boardinghouse for single girls; a forbidden pilgrimage to the Holy Land. Each time, the cataclysmic event has the same effect. It forces the reexamination of circumstances long since taken for granted; it forces the protagonists to confront the terms of their existence.

[3]

Muriel Spark was born in Edinburgh in 1918. Her father Jewish, her mother Presbyterian, she was educated in the latter faith, an unlikely beginning for one of England's more important contemporary Catholic writers. Like Joyce's feelings for dear, dirty Dublin, Miss Spark's feelings for the city of her birth are ambivalent:

Edinburgh is the place that I, a constitutional exile, am essentially exiled from. . . . It was Edinburgh that bred within me the conditions of exiledom: and what have I been doing since then but moving from exile to exile? It has ceased to be a fact, it has become a calling. . . . It is a place where I could not hope to be understood. . . . Nevertheless, it is the place where I was first understood.

She arrived in South Africa, her first place of exile, in 1936, married two years later, and had one son, Robin, before her divorce. In South Africa she remained until 1944, when she returned to Britain to do intelligence work at Woburn Abbey, London. After the war, working as a journalist, Miss Spark settled in the city that through years of living in a cultural desert had come to seem the center of the world, but it was not until 1947 that she was able, as editor for the Poetry Society, to find practical use for her developing interest in poetry. A conflict in taste led to the severing of these ties and ultimately, in 1949, the publication of her own magazine, *Forum*.

Derek Stanford joined Miss Spark as co-editor of the second (and final) issue, beginning a literary partnership that lasted until 1956. Books on Wordsworth and Emily Brontë, and collections of the letters of Mary Shelley and Cardinal Newman were the result of this collaboration (as well as a critical study of Miss Spark by Stanford). This was also the period of Miss Spark's most sustained individual efforts as critic and scholar, during which appeared studies of Mary Shelley and John Masefield, and a collection of the Brontë letters, as well as a selection of Emily Brontë's poems.

All the while, however, Miss Spark worked on her own poetry, and in 1952 *The Fanfarlo and Other Verse* was published. The long title poem is a "symbolist ballad" based on some lines in Baudelaire's short story "La Fanfarlo." Narrative and allegorical, the poem anticipates the modes with which Miss Spark will ultimately be most comfortable. It also develops one of her novels' most persistent themes: the inadequacy of a self-indulgent approach to experience. The romantic, Samuel Cramer, in No-Man's Sanitarium, had in life projected his self upon the world; with Dantesque appropriateness, Death offers him neither Heaven nor Hell, either of which would be acceptable, but Limbo, the nonbeing he thoroughly fears. For Miss Spark, as for Hulme and Eliot, it is form, both in art and in life, that brings out what is decent in man. Without strict controls based outside the individual, art disintegrates, life becomes meaningless in the face of death.

Ultimately, the poems of this volume are of limited success, demonstrating that without concentrated, richly suggestive language, even sharp wit and a fine ear for rhythms may not be sufficient. For Miss Spark, the communication of experience is largely dependent on an intricate use of structure and pattern more appropriate to the novel.

In the early fifties, while Miss Spark, reading Beerbohm and Proust, was gradually being converted to prose, a more profound spiritual conversion took place: in 1954 she became a Roman Catholic. Although there is probably no direct relationship between Roman Catholicism and prose, these two conversions are not entirely unrelated. Not the Catholics she knew and met, but rather the prose of John Henry Newman guided her development. "I was put off a long time by individual Catholics, living ones, I mean. Good God, I used to think, if I become a

Catholic, will I grow like them?" This feeling is faithfully reflected in Miss Spark's fiction. While Catholicism itself, its doctrine and structure, outfaces her sharp satire, most of her less pleasant characters are prominently Catholic, treachery their characteristic trait. So strong was Miss Spark's suspicion of individual Catholics, she became first, in 1953, an Anglo-Catholic (attending T. S. Eliot's church), giving herself a kind of period of acclimation as prelude to her final conversion.

From the publication of her first novel, Miss Spark has been placed in the category of "Catholic writers" and has received special attention from this point of view. To a certain extent, her novels invite this approach. One of the most consistent hints of autobiography in her work has been the prevalent Roman Catholic convert as protagonist. In spite of this, Miss Spark would probably deny that she is a "Catholic novelist" in the sense that she writes of specifically Catholic problems, is a spokesman for a doctrine, or seeks in her novels to impose a Catholic view of the world. Catholicism for her has been a source of form and control, "a norm from which one can depart." It is the framework within which one can find freedom and individuality. "Nobody can deny that I speak with my own voice as a writer now, whereas before I was never sure what I was, the ideas teemed but I couldn't sort them out, I was talking and writing with other people's voices. But not any longer." The novels support Miss Spark's assertion of independence. Her characters are never shown in search of an absolute morality, a truth that exists prior to and independent of themselves. They seek rather their own identities, their own special relationships to reality. Values, in Miss Spark's world, are meaningful only when realized in terms of human experience.

Muriel Spark's "The Seraph and the Zambesi" won the *Observer* short story contest in 1951. Even then, however, she was far from thinking of herself as a novelist. When, in 1954, Alan MacLean of Macmillan's suggested she do a novel for them, she still thought it "an inferior way of writing." However, taking up the idea, she retreated to a small cottage in Allington, and in 1957 *The Comforters* was finally completed and published.

This is a book about obsessions: Caroline Rose, recent convert to Catholicism, at work on a study entitled *Form in the Modern Novel*, is obsessed by voices that seem to be narrating a novel in which she is a character; Laurence Manders, her former lover, is obsessed by the mysterious, probably criminal activities of his grandmother, Louisa Jepp; Willi Stock (the Baron), owner of a bookshop across from Foyle's, is obsessed with the notion that Mervyn Hogarth, one of Grandma Jepp's associates, is the foremost diabolist in England. In fact each of the significant characters in this novel is driven by his own peculiar singleness of vision and purpose.

The implications of this obsessiveness are complex. Most obvious, perhaps, is the breakdown of communication between individuals immersed in private worlds; the very title of the novel, referring to the comforters of Job, suggests the inability of anyone to understand anyone else's predicament. Aware of her companions' retreats into "private obsession," as well as her own, Caroline sees a world of "courteous maniacs discreetly making allowances for everyone else's derangement." The broken plaster saints of the Hogarths, for example, are for Laurence the key to his grandmother's smuggling ring, for the Baron proof of sacrilegious ceremonies, for Caroline evidence of a contrived plot being put together by the mysterious writer. Caroline, Laurence, and the Baron examine the same fragments of reality; but the *Weltansicht* of each is distinct. Clearly these obsessions do not yield the same degrees of accuracy. Laurence's picture of things as they are is reasonably sound, as far as it goes; the Baron's is manifestly false. And Caroline's assumption of another plane of existence is, like most of the uncanny occurrences in Miss Spark's work, beyond corroboration.

In following through their preoccupations, all of the protagonists in one way or another distort the nature of reality. However, in so doing they create a reality of their own, they imaginatively extend the "real" world; and this, for Muriel Spark, who, in an interview with Frank Kermode, referred to the writing of a novel as itself a kind of obsession, is precisely the function of the artist. Each man is, in fact, an artist in so far as he gives form to the flux in which he is immersed, each vision of the world is to a certain extent valid. However, since some artists are better than others, distinctions must be made. The Baron's fanaticism limits his view of the world, as does Laurence's cold objectivity. Only Caroline's world remains open to possibility; and she does in fact end by writing a novel.

But if obsessiveness has aesthetic as well as psychological implications, it also, in *The Comforters*, has its theological aspects. The most bizarre variety of religious experience in the novel is the Baron's perverse and all-consuming interest in Diabolism. Miss Spark is not here interested in the details of Diabolism, she describes no Black Mass. The Baron's passion is developed solely in terms of his investigations of Mervyn Hogarth. This is perfectly in keeping with the novel as a whole, which is epistemological rather than ontological, concerned with the process of knowing rather than the nature of what is known.

The book's most sophisticated analysis of religious knowing, however, concerns not the Baron but Caroline Rose. A recent convert, she is curiously free of speculation about Church dogma; she confines her thoughts to the position of the Catholic in English society, and the unpleasantness of individual Catholics, chiefly Georgina Hogg. But she is extremely anxious to learn the nature and identity of the mysterious voices. Seeking, like Job, news of the supernatural, she turns to the Baron, Father Jerome, who had instructed her in Catholicism, and Laurence, for comfort. Their responses are characteristic: the Baron thinks she is mad, but does not care as long as she will listen to his own preoccupations; Father Jerome does not know whether the voices are delusion or not, but feels that morally this is of secondary importance; and Laurence, detached and observant, tries unsuccessfully to capture the voices on a tape recorder. Caroline herself speculates inconclusively on the possible identity of the higher Novelist—she alone is convinced there is one—considering Satan, a woman, a hermaphrodite, and a Holy Soul in Purgatory. But this problem is soon lost in graver concerns. If Caroline is being written into the novel, does the Novelist then control her actions along with those of the others in the "plot"? The premise correct, this conclusion is distinctly possible.

Caroline's resistance to the thought increases in proportion to her sense of being manipulated. When Laurence guesses at a relationship between Georgina Hogg and the Hogarths, she comments:

"I can see clearly that your mind is working under the pressure of someone else's necessity, and under the suggestive power of some irresponsible writer you are allowing yourself to become an amateur sleuth in a cheap mystery piece."

Clearly implied is the analogy between the writer's relation to his characters and God's to man. Although Caroline's concerns are pointedly non-Catholic through most of the book, she is indirectly involved in one of the knottiest of theological problems, the conflict of fate and free will, the pain of living under the "pressure of someone else's necessity." That God in this metaphor should appear as an "irresponsible writer" suggests that Caroline, like Job, has limited perception, and may not fully understand the nature of things.

[9]

A passage near the novel's conclusion is pertinent: "Her sense of being written into the novel was painful. Of her constant influence on its course she remained unaware and now she was impatient for the story to come to an end, knowing that the narrative could never become coherent to her until she was at last outside it, and at the same time consummately inside it." In one sense, this is an assertion by Miss Spark that there is an interaction between herself and her characters, who take on a life of their own. But it is also an indication that Caroline's life is less thoroughly determined than she thinks; and the final phrase at least suggests that the ways of God, and man's relation to God, can be expressed only in terms of a paradox, and are knowable only mystically.

Ultimately, Caroline, who is indeed called a "mystic" by her friends, collects notes on the voices' dictations and, piecing together the hypothetical novel, seems to become the Novelist; she is now both inside and outside. Even so, her view of the truth is not absolute. Laurence, who finds he dislikes being a character in a novel as much as Caroline did, claims that Caroline, "martyred by misunderstanding," herself understands nobody, "for instance the Baron, my father, myself." Of Laurence and the Baron I have already spoken. Edwin, Laurence's father, represents the utterly contemplative religious man who, having withdrawn from practical affairs, can no longer cope with them. In short, we are back again to mutually exclusive obsessions: the rational materialist, the contemplative, the diabolist, and the mystic, perceiving the world in their own ways, cannot communicate.

Laurence suggests the only way out of the impasse when, writing to Caroline of mutual misunderstanding, he insists that he nonetheless loves her. But instead of sending the note, he rips it up.

All in all, this book, endorsing multiplicity of perspective, is a surprising work for a recent convert to the faith. Catholics are here hypocritical and treacherous, like the Hogg woman, ineffectual, like Edwin Manders, or at best well meaning but limited in their ability to understand, like Father Jerome. And even if we read the novel allegorically, with Caroline representing mystical knowing, Miss Spark carefully cuts the ground from under us; Caroline's insight has psychological as well as spiritual roots. Her disgust at Hogg's breasts (her own sins of the flesh are described as "fastidious"), her careful wiping off of the Baron's light kiss, her spraying of a room with germicide after Hogg has been there, all suggest a limiting obsessiveness. Here is the real paradox: in order to see the world intensely enough to "extend it imaginatively," it is necessary to distort it, to seize upon selected perceptions of reality. Caroline's view may be the most satisfying aesthetically, but it is not the final view.

The Comforters is a book not simply about the novelist's ways of knowing the world; it is also a study of ways of expressing this knowledge, "a novel to work out the technique." Miss Spark is a witty writer; and it is one of her finest self-critical accomplishments that she is very much aware of the dangers of being excessively witty. Caroline accuses the Novelist of using the "phoney plot" of a "cheap mystery piece." And of the novel's most Dickensian creation, Georgina Hogg, she comments, "Not a real-life character, only a gargoyle." Caroline is correct in each case, but her awareness, since she herself becomes the Novelist, helps offset the criticism. Limiting her scope, Miss Spark insures a limited success. Her characters are shallow, brought to the appearance of life by a gimmick; but the gimmick is effective, the appearance *is*, at least evanescently, there.

If *The Comforters* is an epistemological novel, emphasizing man's relation to the external world, *Robinson* (1958) turns

[11]

inward and analyzes the nature of the self. The narrative line is simple enough: January Marlow is one of three survivors of a plane that crashes on Robinson's island, where they are forced to wait three months for the arrival of the pomegranate boat. Tension among them grows until, a month before the boat is due, Robinson disappears, apparently the victim of a brutal and bloody murder. Mutual suspicion adds to the strain; but just when it seems still another murder is inevitable, Robinson calmly reappears. The survivors are rescued, and January reads in the paper the next year that the island is slowly sinking into the sea.

Suggestions of allegory, a possibility in *The Comforters*, are here, as pointed out by Carol Ohmann's perceptive study, insistent. On the novel's first page we are told that the island, were it not for certain tangible evidence, would seem "a time and landscape of the mind," "an apocryphal island" that "resembles a locality of childhood, both dangerous and lyrical." Also insisted upon is the island's resemblance to a human being, so striking that various regions have been named for parts of the body. Even the inner man is suggested by a seething volcano ("The Furnace") and a system of secret tunnels.

The protagonists themselves have certain characteristics of the human psyche. January Marlow, the narrator (whose name suggests Conrad's explorations of dark inner boundaries), is in a sense the total self, the battleground on which all conflicts take place. She has lost her husband and gone through some undescribed crisis that led to her joining the Catholic Church; her resolution of the problem tentative at best, the plane crash is her emotional crack-up.

The three men seem to correspond to the fragmented parts of January's mind, wrenched out of a superficially harmonious relationship by the crash. Tommy Wells, editor of *Your Future* magazine, always associated with the irrational, with magical

[12]

thinking, and easily the most violent of the three, has many of the qualities of the Id. Robinson, authoritarian and repressive, a Catholic purist intent on controlling January's sexual and religious life, has much in common with the Superego. And Jimmie, easy-going, actually related to Robinson but always trying to temper the conflicts between his cousin and Wells, makes a reasonable Ego. Miguel, a young orphan adopted by Robinson, is less neatly placeable in the Freudian scheme. He, rather than January, is the object of a struggle for attention among the men. He is in fact (in addition to corresponding to January's own son) a kind of childhood equivalent to January.

If the three men can be understood as divisions of the mind, they function equally well as possible varieties of religious experience. Wells, bearer of magic charms and totems, clearly represents a primitive response to reality; Jimmie, far less "obsessed," is a more conventional Catholic layman; Miles Mary Robinson, however, is of the greatest interest. A student for the priesthood, he became a deacon but finally left the Church in his hatred of worship of the Virgin, which forms the subject of his book, *Dangers of the Marian Doctrine*. January analyzes his obsession in this way: "Mariology was identified with Earth mythology, both were identified with superstition, and superstition with evil." Theologically as well as psychologically, Robinson and Wells are opposites.

The crucial question, of course, involves January's relation to these three men, to these fragments of her mind. Superficially, she is irritated, perhaps frustrated, by Robinson, attracted by Jimmie, although contemptuous of his ineffectuality, and thoroughly repelled by Wells. However, her reactions to Wells in particular are ambivalent. When, for example, Robinson plays a Rossini opera on the phonograph, Wells and January band together to discuss cabaret. "My word," Wells finally concludes, as Robinson frowns, "we've got a lot in common, you and I." The link is profound. January, whose name hints an intimate tie to the natural world, is herself obsessed by the desire to worship the moon, a pagan goddess associated by Robinson with Mariology; and in spite of Robinson's violent objections, she persists in teaching Miguel the Rosary. Against her conscious beliefs, then, January often prefers Id to Superego, superstition to "higher" religious forms. The breakdown (or plane crash) has left her especially vulnerable, her defenses are down, her darker purposes are near the surface. And when Robinson disappears, when, in other words, all repression is gone, she is forced to confront the destructive possibilities long buried within her.

The results are nearly catastrophic. Wells first attempts to blackmail Jimmie, then to destroy the journal of "facts" January has been compiling, and finally to kill January while she is, appropriately enough, exploring the depths of the tunnels in search of Robinson. When Robinson, reappeared, is told of what has happened, he remarks simply, "It was only to be expected." And indeed, with Superego withdrawn, and Ego ineffectual, it is only to be expected that the urges of the Id, which have no principle of self-preservation, will threaten January's very existence. And it is also to be expected that once relieved of the critical judgment that censors the appeal of the "superstitious" aspects of Catholicism, January will drift closer and closer to primitive religious experience, to a way of magical thinking that ultimately offers only the refuge of a self-created fantasy world, and none of the spiritual awareness of a more sophisticated approach to reality.

What has been described so far is a clever but possibly sterile representation of the workings of a human mind; allegory, essentially static and presupposing a rigid universality of experience, is for good reason a mode rare in contemporary

[14]

literature. But the mind explored in *Robinson* is not that of humanity in general, but rather that of a specific individual with a particular set of experiences that have brought her to her present crisis. And what prevents *Robinson* from forming a self-enclosed allegorical system are the frequent references to January's past, to the life that has resulted in breakdown. This life, suggestively but incompletely described, gives the novel its sense of reality.

January Marlow is one of three sisters. Her older sister, Agnes, is married to Ian Brodie, a doctor, violently anti-Marian, whom January often compares to Robinson, while her younger sister, Julia, has married a bookie, Curly Lonsdale, who strongly resembles Tom Wells. In January's mind, Ian and Curly fight for the soul of her teenage son, Brian, just as Wells and Robinson struggle over Miguel. Wondering who is taking care of Brian while she is on the island, she hopes "it was Curly, whom I could never, myself, take to." What she consciously denies herself, she wishes for her son; Miguel corresponds not simply to Brian but to January herself.

It is now possible to piece together the full world of *Robinson*. January Marlow, married about fifteen or sixteen years before the action of the novel, lost her husband after six months of marriage and the conception of one child. In a long search for some kind of shape and significance in her life, she emerges finally, within a year of the crash, a Catholic. But rather than putting an end to her spiritual quest, conversion brings on a crisis. Miss Spark's remarks about her own life—the dates of her marriage, the birth of her son, and her conversion conspicuously parallel January's—will be instructive here:

I decided at last to become a Catholic, by which time I really became very ill. I was going about, but I was ready for a breakdown. . . . I had a feeling while I was undergoing this real emotional suffering that it was all part of the conversion.

The analysis of similar post-conversion suffering is the subject of *Robinson*. In her commitment to Catholicism, January is faced with giving up, or at least placing under strict control, her "lower," instinctive drives, including, presumably, fleshly desires, and her superstitious tendencies, which infantilely look to religion as magic rather than as a demanding discipline.

The return of Robinson represents a kind of psychic reintegration, made possible by the descent into the tunnels, the dark inner recesses of the self, where January encounters Wells while searching for Robinson. Wells, armed with a knife, has January trapped when she flashes on her light, temporarily blinding him, and escapes. The significance is clear. By shedding light on the dark corners of her mind, by self-understanding, she reachieves health.

As cleverly as *Robinson* is wrought, its success is limited in that its finest qualities are understood rather than felt. Like *The Comforters* self-consciously formal, *Robinson* solves technical problems and tests a framework within which the turmoil of emotional upheavals can be expressed in controlled form, and helps establish the basis for future work.

Miss Spark's next book, *The Go-Away Bird and Other Stories* (1958), collects her shorter fiction. These stories, not always as impressive as her longer works, demonstrate a sharp wit, precise visual sense, and an ear for dialogue and the rhythms of speech. But they lack the qualities crucial in her novels: complex patterns of action, repetition and variation of central themes. Since these techniques depend on length, it is not surprising that the book's best piece, "The Go-Away Bird," is also its longest.

This story, which gets its name from "the subtle voice of the

[16]

grey-crested lourie, commonly known as the go-away bird by its call, 'go'way, go'way,' " is in some ways Miss Spark's finest achievement to that point in her career. As Derek Stanford has pointed out, "Much of Muriel Spark's fiction is an imaginative denial of her roots." Here, the heroine, Daphne du Toit, brought up in South Africa, and forced by the war to stay longer than she likes, first rejects her homeland in favor of the promised land of London, which, finding it equally lacking, she then rejects in turn. Returning to South Africa, she is murdered as a result of an old family feud, ironically by a man too senile to be considered dangerous.

A rejector of roots, Daphne is herself rejected. Haunted by the cry of the grey-crested lourie in South Africa, by the unwanted talking budgerigar—who repeatedly shouts, "Go'way, go to hell"—in England, she finds no acceptance as a human being in either of her worlds. Her uncle Chakata, who brings her up, and Old Tuys, who murders her, both regard her as an object of contention in their feud; her lover, novelist Ralph Mercer, simply uses her to fulfill his needs. Her humanity unrecognized, she is in reality dead before Old Tuys pulls the trigger. In a world that turns people into objects, she lacks the strength to forge an existence of her own; unlike those of Caroline Rose and January Marlow, her crisis leads not to rebirth but to extinction.

In the novel, Miss Spark has theorized, the author must be obsessed by a given point of view. In *Memento Mori,* her obsession is the aged. Almost all of the important characters are over seventy; many are in their eighties.

The novel's premise is simple: the elderly protagonists one by one receive mysterious phone calls with substantially the same message: "Remember you must die." The voice differs, depending upon the recipient; it may be strong and sinister, a civil young man's, a Teddy-boy's, an old man's, or, in one case, even a woman's. The caller or callers are never identified; but two of the most rational characters in the novel, ex-police inspector Mortimer and former servant Jean Taylor, both think the caller to be Death. More significant, however, than the kind of voice heard by each individual, more important even than the actual identity of the caller, are the distinct reactions to the message. What distinguishes one man from another is not the fact that he must die—all share this—but rather his attitude toward this ultimate limitation: whether, like the large group headed by Dame Lettie Colston and her brother Godfrey, he is shaken by the grim reminder, or whether, like Alec Warner, Charmion Colston, Jean Taylor, and ex-Inspector Mortimer, he takes it in his stride.

Dame Lettie, most frantic of those deeply affected by the phone calls, devotes all her energies to seeking the identity of the caller. Paranoically certain that the relatives and friends mentioned in her will are trying to frighten her, she ignores the message itself. When she does die, she is unprepared, and has in fact spent her last years in terror; by not having confronted the fact of her death, she has not lived. Lettie's brother, and the rest in this group, evade reality in much the same way, if less desperately. But there is more variety among those who face death with equanimity.

Dr. Alec Warner, a sociologist, has in the nine years since his seventieth birthday intensively studied the problems of old age with the aid of a complicated system of notebooks and index cards. Formerly Jean Taylor's lover, he is now the completely objective, detached observer, amiable but obsessed with data. He delights in delivering extremely good or bad news to his peers, asking always that they record their pulse and temperature. Characteristically, he responds to his own mysterious call by indexing his physical reactions. This scientific detachment provides a means of coming to terms with the human condition. But its impersonality eliminates fear at the cost of eliminating all emotion, of eliminating a good part of one's humanity. More than that: this intellectualization of experience is vulnerable. When fire destroys Warner's notes, he himself is for all practical purposes destroyed.

Charmion Colston, Roman Catholic convert, is a once popular novelist grown senile. However, when her novels suddenly become fashionable, her mental powers reintegrate; and, while assuring her mysterious caller that she has indeed thought often of her death, she assumes the call is from a journalist wishing to interview her. An artist, she has incorporated the call into the world of her obsession, and, though she confronts death, she distorts the encounter. Miss Spark is careful to show that Charmion's way of life, while better than most, is as imperfect as her attitude toward death.

As a writer, Charmion seems spokesman for Miss Spark, and, in a conversation with Guy Leet, echoes her creator's own position: "The art of fiction is very like the practice of deception." The notion that art is deception, a supreme fiction, is at the heart of Miss Spark's aesthetic. But Guy Leet makes a crucial shift in perspective when he asks, "Is the practice of deception in life an art too?" To which Charmion replies, "In life, everything is different. Everything is in the Providence of God." But Charmion's weakness lies in the fact that she does practice the art of deception in her life.

Both she and her husband, Godfrey, have had extramarital affairs many years in the past; but while Charmion knows of Godfrey's, Godfrey knows neither of Charmion's nor that Charmion knows of his. This moral blackmail has kept Godfrey in fear of his wife throughout their marriage, and makes possible a more conventional threat of blackmail by Mrs. Pettigrew (an older version of the Hogg woman). Visibly shaken by exposure, Charmion becomes tired where she once was energetic; Godfrey is filled with new vigor. The entire relationship pivots on this lie, and reveals the flaw in Charmion's approach to experience: she has mixed art with life rather than carefully using one to shed light on the other; she has confused the power of the artist with the power of God.

Closer to the novel's moral center is Jean Taylor. Once Charmion's maid, she converted to Catholicism after her mistress, but is now more serious-minded in her beliefs. Miss Taylor herself receives no phone call; an occupant of the Maud Long Medical Ward (for aged women), she is provided with her own *memento mori* by the introduction of advanced geriatric cases into the ward. Not at all upset, she tells Alec Warner she is probably a gerontologist at heart. And when Lettie tells her of the phone calls, Taylor replies: "In my belief, the author of the anonymous telephone calls is Death himself, as you might say. . . . If you don't remember Death, Death reminds you to do so."

It is as easy to identify Taylor with Miss Spark's moral side as it is Charmion with her aesthetic. Taylor is indeed given the novel's last word; she "lingered for a time, employing her pain to magnify the Lord, and meditating confidingly upon Death, the first of the Four Last Things to be remembered." However, there is a suggestion in *Memento Mori*, not entirely absent from these last lines, that Taylor, who in a youthful discussion with Warner had cited graveyards as proof that people exist, is perhaps too ready not simply to have death in mind but to exclude life. And like those of most of Miss Spark's Catholics, Taylor's actions are not beyond question. Her decision to reveal Charmion's infidelities, while made in Godfrey's interest, is nonetheless a betrayal—"There is a time for loyalty and a time when loyalty comes to an end"—and a perhaps inappropriately Godlike act of manipulation.

It is typical of Miss Spark that her most likable character,

[20]

the one who most humanly expresses her point of view, is not closely linked to the facts of her own life, is not even a religious figure. *Memento Mori*'s crucial speech is delivered by Henry Mortimer, the first to suspect Death as the caller, who firmly denies a specifically religious perspective:

"If I had my life over again I should form the habit of nightly composing myself to thoughts of death. I would practise, as it were, the remembrance of death. There is no other practise which so intensifies life. Death, when it approaches, ought not to take one by surprise. It should be part of the full expectancy of life. Without an ever-present sense of death life is insipid. You might as well live on the white of eggs."

It is Mortimer's point of view, not necessarily religious but compatible with religion, that informs the entire novel. Death, which seems the crowning absurdity of human existence, the final irony, is precisely that which defines life, gives it significance. Human action, which would in fact be absurd in the context of eternal life, becomes meangingful precisely because it is limited by death; time gains importance because it is irredeemable. To live without awareness of death is to live in bad faith, in deception, to deprive oneself of the only opportunity to rescue existence from absurdity, to forge being in the place of nonbeing. At no point does Miss Spark more clearly express the existential perspective implied in so much of her work.

It should be made clear, however, that *Memento Mori* is not simply about death, but old age as well. Miss Spark, like Gulliver viewing the Struldbrugs, finds not wisdom based on a wealth of experience but rather an intensification of human folly. This sense of the ridiculous is produced by the refusal of even those who obviously have little time to live to act as if they were not going to live forever; instead of choosing values that resist the effects of age and death, they pursue precisely those goals most vulnerable to passing time. Godfrey Colston keeps the niece of his friend to exercise what remains of his sexual urges, eagerly watching her skirt raised above her garter (until Mrs. Pettigrew fulfills his limited objectives more cheaply); poet Percy Mannering and critic Guy Leet engage in near lethal combat over the latter's remarks about Ernest Dowson, the struggle mitigated only by the feebleness of the participants; Eric Colston and his father, Godfrey, engage in a less physical but bitterer conflict that has pointlessly lasted fifty years. Miss Spark has it both ways. She directly satirizes the ineffectual old, who can no longer even indulge their vices; but her ultimate target is man in his prime, who no less absurdly dedicates himself to self-defeating ends.

Technically, *Memento Mori* is most remarkable for the large number of important characters to whom Miss Spark manages to give life in the brief space of 224 pages. She draws sharply and well (several critics have labeled her powers of delineation Dantesque), and while her eccentrics may still have something of the gargoyle about them, the reader now has the sense of what Guy Leet calls a character's "secret life"—they retain enough mystery to seem possible. And here, her wit, which is rarely boisterously funny, but rather depends upon a quick sense of the grotesque, is shown to its best advantage in the macabre context. In short, Miss Spark is able for the first time to temper the needs of her techniques to the work as a whole; the results are impressive.

In *The Ballad of Peckham Rye* (1960), the focus of attention seems to be Dougal Douglas, the diabolical Edinburgh Arts man, who apparently offers freedom and life, but is really the bearer of death and destruction. Hired by Meadows, Meade, and Grindley, manufacturers of nylon textiles, "to bring vision into the lives of the workers"—he later takes an identical position for rival company Drover Willis, under the name Douglas

Dougal—he ultimately creates a general ferment in the community that subsides only upon his departure.

Hints as to Dougal's real nature are scattered throughout the novel and emphasized by Dougal himself. Obviously deformed by his humpback, he has a less noticeable physical peculiarity that he gleefully shares with his friends: two bumps on either side of his head, remains of horns he claims were shaved off by a plastic surgeon. And Dougal is also delighted to talk of dreams in which he appears as the Devil.

But Dougal's identity is ambiguous. Although he insists it is not incompatible with being a devil, he claims powers of exorcism, the ability to drive devils out of people. And, walking through a cemetery with Merle Coverdale, he poses "like an angel-devil, with his hump shoulder and gleaming smile." It is no easier to know whether he is angel or devil than to know whether he is Dougal Douglas or Douglas Dougal.

This ambiguity envelops Dougal. His "fatal flaw"—he insists everybody has one—his inability to tolerate sickness, is evidence both of a limited sense of compassion and of a commitment to health and life. The marriage that Dougal's counsel and example temporarily prevents would tie Humphrey Place to the penny-pinching, materialistic Dixie, and deprive him of all spiritual freedom. Even the murder of Miss Coverdale by Humphrey's employer, Mr. Druce, is not caused by Dougal's will toward evil, but rather by the inability of the lovers to reject the deadly pattern of life on which they have become dependent. In fact, Dougal's chief antagonists are a collection of hoodlums, a strange bunch for the devil to be at odds with.

Dougal himself is neither good nor evil, neither angel nor devil (which is the same as saying he is both); he represents simply a force, a source of energy which takes on moral significance in relation to people, in this case the community of

Peckham Rye. For in spite of Dougal's fascination, the community is the true focus of the novel. Angel or devil, Dougal is simply the cataclysmic event in the novel that jolts reality into a new perspective.

He is also the analyst of Peckham Rye's four types of morality:

"Take the first category, Emotional. Here, for example, it is considered immoral for a man to live with a wife who no longer appeals to him. Take the second, Functional, in which the principal factor is class solidarity such as, in some periods and places, has also existed amongst the aristocracy, and of which the main manifestation these days is the trade union movement. Three, Puritanical, of which there are several modern variants, monetary advancement being the most prevalent gauge of the moral life in this category. Four, Traditional, which accounts for about one per cent of the Peckham population, and which in its simple form is Christian."

The characters of *Ballad* illustrate Dougal's categories: Emotional, Mr. Druce, whose wife is "narrow-minded"; Functional, the office typists, jealous of Miss Coverdale's special relationship to management; Puritanical, chiefly Dixie, who will do anything to save money, but who feels no guilt sleeping with Humphrey whenever she can. Of the traditionally moral, there are no examples. What the first three moral types have in common is their response to human beings as objects subordinate to other concerns.

Dougal's own approach to experience seems anything but "Traditional." Unable to tolerate other people's illnesses, advising unrestrained absenteeism in the workers, urging uninhibited expression of inner feelings, he apparently carries self-indulgence to its furthest extremes. However, Dougal's beliefs resist systemization. What he offers is freedom from the confines of artificial moralities; he preaches the respect for oneself that must precede respect for others. But this is as far as he goes. He suggests no discipline with which to shape this freedom; he evades the necessity of respect for others. And freedom without discipline, a sense of Self without a sense of the Other, can be psychologically and morally devastating.

The suggestion is that few can survive true freedom. Most are dependent on unreal systems of behavior; but as with the boarders at Harry Hope's in *The Iceman Cometh*, for most of Peckham Rye confrontation of reality leads not to liberation but to disintegration. Deprived of their props, they fall. Mr. Druce and Miss Coverdale are most thoroughly destroyed by their new perspective, and Humphrey Place is uprooted and confused. Dixie Morse, however, though jilted, is relatively unshaken; smug and certain, she survives.

Dougal himself, a moral catalyst, has other specific functions in Miss Spark's world. It is the artist's job, she has said, to show us the truth, even if he must lie to do it. One of Dougal's numerous occupations is ghost-writing the biography of retired actress and singer Maria Cheeseman. A good artist rather than a mere reporter, Dougal lies incessantly, fabricating from his own experience and that of people he meets the "true" story of poor old Cheese, who ends less than completely certain of the boundaries between illusion and reality.

The artist's traditional estrangement from society is given full play by Miss Spark. Dougal captivates some, but most view him with suspicion and hatred, question his manhood and his decency, and actually stalk and hound him. The nature of society's hatred for the artist is probed almost allegorically, in a manner suggestive of *Robinson*.

Dougal's chief antagonist is Trevor Lomas, suitor of Dixie, and leader of the conspiracy against Dougal. Trevor has, to be sure, some specific reasons for hating Dougal, whose deformities seem particularly attractive to Trevor's girl friend, significantly named Beauty; but Trevor's feelings consist mainly of blind, irrational hatred and fear. He steals Dougal's notebooks —just as Wells steals January's notebooks in *Robinson*—and is further infuriated by the fact that he cannot understand them. The final confrontation occurs in the newly excavated tunnel near the police station, when Dougal is leaving Peckham for a new career, selling tape recorders to African witch doctors. Dougal fends Trevor off, with the aid of dexterity made possible by his deformity, and by shining a light in his face. The relation of this scene to the climax of *Robinson* is evident, and surely not accidental. Ignorance, fear, animal desire: in each case, these are the enemies of freedom, of self-expression; these are the enemies of the artist.

The Bachelors (1960), like *Memento Mori*, is a clear instance of fiction as obsession. This novel is almost completely populated by unmarried men and women. However, as is usually the case in Miss Spark's work, the specific evokes the universal; the characters are bachelors in the sense of people alone, searching for union with other men, or with something larger than themselves.

In *The Bachelors* there are two distinct poles of interest: Patrick Seton and Ronald Bridges. Seton is a medium on trial for fraudulent conversion. Alice, his mistress, a diabetic, is pregnant with his child and wishes to marry him. Seton, seeing this as an encumbrance, looks forward to his acquittal so that he can take his fiancée to the continent and "liberate her spirit" with an overdose of insulin. Bridges, an epileptic, and a Catholic, operates a handwriting museum, and is often called upon by the police as an expert witness in his specialty. At Seton's trial, he denounces the spiritualist as a forger.

It would seem that Bridges and Seton have little in common; but actually they are, in the mode of Dostoevsky and Conrad, doubles. Diabolical overtones (a carry-over from *Ballad*) are present in both: Seton, fiendish in his plot against Alice, probably pronounces his name Satan; and even virtuous Ronald, as epileptic, is alternately envisioned as possessed by the devil, or suffering the devil's revenge. The resemblance goes further. Seton's spiritualistic trances precisely resemble Ronald's fits, so that when Ronald does have a seizure during the trial, the judge, saturated with the world of spiritualism, desperately asks, "Is this man a medium?"

The diabolical connotations are not at all limited to Seton and Bridges. Matthew Finch, Bridge's Jesuit-trained friend, calls all spiritualists heretics because they are dualists who refuse to recognize a morality of the flesh. (He is thinking specifically of Seton's reluctance to marry Alice.) He then, surprisingly, expands this category of heretics to include all bachelors: "I'm afraid we are heretics, or at least possessed by devils. . . . It shows a dualistic attitude, not to marry if you aren't going to be a priest or a religious. You've got to affirm the oneness of reality in some form or another." Bridges points out that this is theologically inaccurate, but Finch insists. Sinning against the unity of being, all bachelors are kinds of devils; and that which is diabolical in human life is thereby defined as separation—from God, from nature, from man, and, in a world of people with only the vaguest hold on identity, from oneself.

It is not, however, Matthew Finch who is the prophet of this world of devils; his understanding is intellectual rather than emotional. It is rather Ronald Bridges who is given the final word, contemplating the bachelors of London: "fruitless souls, crumbling tinder, like his own self which did not bear thinking of. But it is all demonology, he thought, and he brought them all to witness, in his old style, one by one before the courts of his mind. . . . It is all demonology and to do with creatures of the air." Ronald, who, were he not disabled by the disease of the possessed, would have been a priest, suffers most keenly from the torments of separation. But it is precisely because of his pain that he is also most directly aware of the mechanism of grace. As Ronald points out, when Matthew concedes that a heretical attitude is part of original sin, "The Christian economy seems to be so ordered that original sin is necessary to salvation." The greatest good proceeds from evil; the Fall, separation from God and nature, is necessary to man's redemption.

But awareness, like freedom, is hard to bear. A passage from Philippians, a "charm to ward off the disgust, despair, and brainburning," frequently runs through Ronald's mind: "All that rings true, all that commands reverence, and all that makes for right; all that is pure, all that is lovely, all that is gracious in the telling; virtue and merit, wherever virtue and merit are found—let this be the argument of your thoughts." Surrounded by demons, Ronald must penetrate the possessed world and arrive at the true nature of things, to find truth in a world of devilish deception. Like *The Comforters*, *The Bachelors* explores ways of knowing; and Patrick Seton, in communication with the spirit world, and Ronald Bridges, student of the material manifestation of human personality, are, like the artist, high priests of the investigation of the nature of reality.

But Seton, a remarkably sound medium—only one or two personal enemies even pretend to question his legitimacy here —lacks unity of being. The fraudulent conversion and forged letter are simply the last in a long series of similar offenses; his relation to worldly existence is completely false. The trial itself is taken by many, notably Seton and Alice, as a "test of God." Seton, certain of acquittal, sees it as proof of God's acquiescence in his plan to liberate Alice's spirit; and Alice, convinced of Seton's innocence, and of his love for her, views the trial as a test of God's justice. When her lover is found guilty, she says, "I don't believe in God." The verdict, which saves her life, is, in fact, surprising testimony to the presence of justice in the world. However, Miss Spark emphasizes its unexpectedness, and, as we have seen, leaves Ronald in a city of demons. The triumph of truth is apparently rare.

The Bachelors is, after all, a kind of symphony of deceptions. Seton has beguiled Freda Flower. But his prosecutor, Martin Bowles, is in a similar relationship to client Isobel Billows; he is in fact just barely "on the right side of the law." Father Socket and his homosexual partner, the clairvoyant Mike Garland, are con men who run a cinema showing Nudies and featuring live girls who entertain afterwards. Dr. Lyte is in mortal terror of Seton, who has, without knowing the details, stumbled on an illicit operation in the respectable doctor's past. This is, in short, a world in which fraud is rampant, in which the holy is corrupt, in which innocence is largely illusory. The alternatives to sinking into the mire are to retreat from the world entirely, as Ronald's former mistress, Hildegarde, does—becoming first a spiritualist, then a Catholic convert, and finally a nun—or to keep Philippians firmly in mind, as Ronald himself does. "There are," says Ronald at one point, "only two religions, the spiritualist and the Catholic." There are only the world of devils and the world of God; and although the two are in eternal conflict, they are apparently intimately related.

A word should be said about Miss Spark's psychology of bachelorhood. As usual, she courts the stereotype, but ends by deflating it. "I suppose most people would say the confirmed bachelor is a subconscious homosexual," Matthew Finch offers. "They say all bachelors are queers. Hee hee. Or motherfixated or something." "Impossible to prove," Ronald replies. "You can only deduce homosexuality from facts. Subconscious tendencies, repressions—these ideas are too simple and too tenuous to provide explanations." And in fact there are endless

[29]

reasons for bachelorhood in this world of bachelors, from the overt homosexuality of Father Socket and Mike Garland to the barely repressed effeminacy of Ewart Thorton, from Seton's hatred of society to Ronald Bridges' epilepsy. It is not that Bridges, or Miss Spark, denies the validity of psychoanalytic insight; it is simply that a generalization like Finch's, being true of everybody, sheds no distinguishing light on anyone. Maybe all bachelors—and, possibly, married men—have on some level homosexual tendencies; but Miss Spark chooses to see her characters as individuals rather than as types.

Psychologically as well as morally, then, *The Bachelors* is involved with the problem of correct vision, of true insight; to see God in a world of devils and to see the individual instead of the type are related forms of moral discrimination.

Voices at Play (1961) collects more of Miss Spark's short stories—once again the longest, "Bang-bang You're Dead," is the most successful—and several radio plays, which the author calls "ear-pieces." While Miss Spark's ear for dialogue is flawless, the plays are nonetheless unimpressive; the volume as a whole is further confirmation that we must look to the longer works for Miss Spark's most distinguished achievements.

To this point, Muriel Spark's novels collectively analyze the moral sensibility: ways of knowing the nature of reality (*Comforters* and *Bachelors*), the workings of the self (*Robinson*), limitations inherent in the human condition (*Memento Mori*), and even the classification of ethical responses to experience (*Ballad*). But it is not until *The Prime of Miss Jean Brodie* (1961) that Miss Spark is ready directly to confront the real source of difficulty: the dark moral heart of man.

Jean Brodie, a teacher at Marcia Blaine School for Girls in Edinburgh of the 1930s, is an outspoken woman in her prime (in her case, her forties). She has her own methods of teaching, as well as her own purposes, and gathers around her a group of disciples, who become the "Brodie set": Monica Douglas, famous for mathematics; Rose Stanley, famous for sex; Eunice Gardner, famous for gymnastics and swimming; Jenny Gray, famous for being the prettiest and most graceful of the set; and Sandy Stranger, famous for her vowel sounds, notorious for her small, beady eyes (the only characteristic that has anything at all to do with the real personality of its possessor).

Miss Brodie's teaching is firm, dogmatic, and decidedly eccentric. Incessantly reminding the girls that they are receiving the fruits of her prime, she establishes clear priorities: Art and religion are most important; then philosophy; finally science. But Miss Brodie's profoundest goals are not simply intellectual, not simply the substitution of a personal curriculum for the school's. Her objective is to make of her students the *crème de la crème*. What she means by this phrase is most clearly illustrated by the scene in which Miss Brodie, talking of the glories of Rome, suddenly turns her attention to the window. "Whoever has opened the window has opened it too wide," says Miss Brodie. "Six inches is perfectly adequate. More is vulgar. One should have an innate sense of these things."

Miss Brodie's values, however, go beyond a worship of art and genius and an insistence on the most refined of sensibilities. Politically, she admires Mussolini, who has put an end to unemployment, and she brings from her travels to Italy photographs of marching Fascisti. Firmly against the materialists, Fabians, and pacifists of the faculty, this dualist—for like Patrick Seton, Brodie has divided the world into spirit and matter and assigned herself to the unending defense of the former—goes to Germany to admire Hitler, a prophet-figure like Mussolini, but "more reliable." (Miss Brodie, who herself comes to "power" in the thirties, is repudiated in 1939, and dies just after the war, does finally admit, "Hitler was rather naughty.")

As important to Miss Brodie's pupils as her intellectual, cultural, and political convictions is her private life: her two love affairs and the all-important one that never takes place. First, from the past, subject of fantasy for the set (especially Sandy), is Hugh Carruthers, the scholar killed in battle a week before the Armistice. Contemporary with the Brodie set, however, is Teddy Lloyd, one-armed art teacher and painter, whom Miss Brodie is seen kissing in the art room one day. This was, in her own words, "the great love of her prime." But Lloyd is married and has children, and Miss Brodie renounces him to become mistress of music-teacher Gordon Lowther. However, renunciations of Miss Brodie in her prime are anything but ordinary. When Lloyd has the Brodie girls sit for portraits, which all look like Miss Brodie herself, the teacher becomes obsessed with the idea that her passion for the painter be fulfilled vicariously through Rose Stanley. Famous as she is for sex, however, it is not Rose but pig-eyed Sandy Stranger whom the artist chooses as mistress; and it is on the improbable similarity of Sandy to her mentor that this novel centers.

As we have learned from Patrick Seton and Ronald Bridges, opposites may well be doubles. Nothing in Miss Spark's world breeds antagonism more than essential similarity; and Sandy Stranger, Miss Brodie's stand-in, is also her betrayer. Miss Brodie, by virtue of her contempt for standard procedures, has always been at odds with Headmistress Mackay, but is beyond her reach until Sandy provides the lever. The reader learns early in the novel that Brodie is betrayed, and halfway through the book the identity of the Judas is revealed; clearly Miss Spark is interested not in building suspense but in exploring the moral significance of the betrayal. Sandy is near the center of consciousness of the novel and, like Kurtz for Marlow, like

[32]

Gatsby for Nick Carraway, Miss Brodie is the means by which Sandy gains insight into herself and the nature of reality.

Sandy does in fact brood continuously on Miss Brodie, first in romanticized fantasies, later, when Brodie is seen kissing Lloyd, with an awareness of adult behavior, and finally, as Miss Brodie hints of her hopes for Rose and Teddy Lloyd, with a strange sense of identification. Sexually, at least for a time, Sandy becomes Miss Brodie.

But the teacher is of more than sexual interest to her most incisive pupil. To the future Sister Helena of the Transfiguration, Brodie's religious posture is crucially important: although "she was by temperament suited only to the Roman Catholic Church," she sees the religion as superstition-ridden, she is firmly anti-Catholic. Here, at least, she is more Scot than Roman, though again in her own way; she goes round to each of the non-Roman churches in the city, rarely missing a Sunday, convinced that whatever her behavior—including her affair with Lowther—God is on her side.

Sandy, like Miss Brodie, is suited to Catholicism; unlike her, she finally does embrace it. And all along, her antipathy toward the non-Catholic, Calvinist atmosphere of Edinburgh is intense. "In fact, it was the religion of Calvin of which Sandy felt deprived, or rather a specified recognition of it. She deserved this birthright; something definite to reject." It is the sense of predestination that most stimulates her, and that links Miss Brodie to the Calvinist approach to experience; and Brodie's manipulations give further play to these feelings. "She thinks she is Providence, thought Sandy, she thinks she is the God of Calvin, she sees the beginning and the end." In one sense, then, Sandy's betrayal of Miss Brodie represents her ultimate success in giving tangible form to the vague feelings she has been longing to reject.

The betrayal itself is given a specifically political context.

Sandy finally decides to act when she discovers that Miss Brodie had talked student Joyce Emily into going to Spain to fight for Franco, in which enterprise the girl was killed. But it is made perfectly clear that this is simply Sandy's pretext. "You won't be able to pin her down on sex," Sandy tells Miss Mackay. "Have you thought of politics?" When the headmistress commends her sudden interest in world affairs, Sandy replies, "I'm not really interested in world affairs, only in putting a stop to Miss Brodie." Superficially political, Sandy's rejection of Brodie is personal. She is not unaware of the value of what her mentor offers: individuality (only the Brodie girls resist the "team" system), self-confidence, and grace in a world that is essentially awkward. But Miss Brodie's social ideal of the *crème de la crème*, her religious sense of the elect, and her attempt to run the lives of her students make her everything Sandy cannot tolerate.

Sandy herself insists there was no betrayal, and tells Miss Brodie (who never learns for certain her betrayer's identity): "If you did not betray us it is impossible that you could have been betrayed by us. The word does not apply." Her final comment is, "It's only possible to betray where loyalty is due." Echoing Jean Taylor, Sandy claims to be acting in behalf of a system of values more significant than the dubious word "loyalty."

However, if Taylor's actions were slightly tainted, Sandy's are far more suspect. Accompanying her like a classical epithet are her sly, beady eyes, which become a fitting symbol when she uses her knowledge of the Brodie-Lloyd relationship as a kind of "moral blackmail" leading to her own affair with Lloyd. As a kind of blackmailer, Sandy enters the company of the villains of each of Miss Spark's previous novels. And Sandy's withdrawal from the world is not completely successful. When visited in the convent, she is always seen tightly clutching the grille; whether this is indicative of her wish to return to the world, or, as the nuns think, of her wish to have no contact with it at all, it is anything but the picture of a soul at peace. Possibly, Sandy's "transfiguration" is a retreat from life rather than a flight to God; meditating frequently on Miss Brodie's sexual activities—she even hits upon the homosexual implications of Brodie's vicarious affair, though she finds this knowledge of little use—Sandy may be sexually motivated in her moral repudiation. In any case, her act remains ambiguous. Has she really rejected Miss Brodie at all; or has she destroyed her only to become her, renouncing worldly life as Brodie renounced Lloyd? Asked of the influences on her treatise, "The Transfiguration of the Commonplace," Sister Helena names only "a Miss Brodie in her prime."

The convincing portrayal of this ambiguity, of the balance of admirable and despicable qualities in Miss Brodie, of the rightness of Sandy's act and its shady motivations, is the achievement of *Jean Brodie*. More effectively than ever before, Miss Spark establishes a core of humanity beneath the ironic surface of her novels. Against a counterpoint of superficial tags—for example: Miss Brodie, "in her prime"; Rose Stanley, "famous for sex"; "pig-eyed" Sandy Stranger—Miss Brodie's complex values and Sandy's ambiguous morals are developed suggestively rather than with stereotypical finality.

Jean Brodie also represents Miss Spark's first full-scale use of the "time shift." The main story line, beginning in the early thirties and reaching its climax with Sandy's betrayal in 1939, alternates with Sandy's memories of her contact with Miss Brodie and the Brodie set during the war, and her present fame as Sister Helena of the Transfiguration. As Frank Kermode has pointed out in another context, in Miss Spark's novels a genuine relation exists between the forms of fiction and the forms of reality. And the manipulations of time indeed

[35]

serve to emphasize the presence of the past, the existential idea that we *are* the sum of our actions (and, most specifically, our decisions). More important, the chronological ordering of events is replaced by a moral order; the emphasis is not on causal sequence, but rather on evaluation *sub specie aeternitatis*.

In *The Girls of Slender Means* (1963), the close relationship of good and evil, important in *Ballad* and *The Bachelors*, implied in the other novels, becomes the book's moral center. This duality, combined in angel-devil Dougal Douglas, split in the double of Patrick Seton–Ronald Bridges, now manifests itself in the changing character of Nicholas Farrington. Beginning as author of the anarchistic and atheistic *Sabbath Notebooks*, Nick becomes a Christian missionary ultimately martyred in Haiti. The novel probes the nature of this "transfiguration."

Opening with a description of London and the May of Teck Club "for the Pecuniary Convenience and Social Protection of Ladies of Slender Means below the age of Thirty Years, who are obliged to reside apart from their Families in order to follow an Occupation in London," the main story line, set at the end of the war, alternates with scenes of Jane Wright, gossip columnist, calling her friends about the martyr's death. These calls, like those in *Memento Mori*, are notable for the reactions of the recipients, each of whom knew Nick at the club, in the days before the catastrophe. Most treat the news as so much more gossip, some would like to know the intimate details of his death; Rudi Bittesch, owner of the *Notebooks* manuscript, speculates on its increased value. Nicholas, who presumably has managed to give meaning to his life, is still perceived superficially by those who knew him; the significance of his actions is not simply beyond understanding but, to them, lacks interest. Only Jane Wright makes an attempt to comprehend the mystery of his conversion, but even she is concerned most with the thoroughness of her "martyr story," and, with the key to the puzzle in her hands, fails to grasp what has happened. This is left to the reader.

At the end of the war, Jane had been assistant to a second-rate publisher, her job consisting chiefly in probing authors' weak points in order to break down their wills and obtain their manuscripts at the lowest possible price. At work on Nicholas Farrington, she brings him to the May of Teck Club, where he meets the girls, especially the poised and beautiful Selina Redwood. Nicholas is soon having an affair with Selina, who is ultimately to have a cataclysmic effect on Nick's life, committing "that action of savagery so extreme that it forced him involuntarily to make an entirely unaccustomed gesture, the signing of the cross upon himself."

This action is initiated by the detonation of an unexploded bomb buried in the Club garden and the resulting fire, which traps many of the girls on the top floor. The skylight, through which they could normally escape, has been sealed off, and the bathroom window is so small and narrow that only the slimmest of girls—like Selina—can make their way out. It is while firemen and volunteers are working frantically to open the skylight before a gas leak brings down the entire building that Nick sees the "savage action": Selina, who had slipped through the window to the roof, suddenly rushes back into the building, apparently in a futile, selfless attempt to help; she soon reappears, weaving her way amid the stunned trapped girls, and climbs through the window with her prized Schiaparelli dress, inspecting it for damage.

The effect on Nick of Selina's inhumanity is brought into focus, first by the actual death in that fire of minister's daughter Joanna Childe, and then, on V-J night, when a seaman, seen only by Nick, stabs the woman with him. Jane Wright later finds a note on Nick's manuscript which, although Jane is unaware of the precise reference, comments on the action: "a vision of evil may be as effective to conversion as a vision of good." In the Christian economy, the devil is an instrument of salvation. Nick's vision of evil is sufficient to shake him from moral indecisiveness. Bisexual, he has always, it seems, had trouble choosing between opposite extremes; his anarchism, which, as Rudi points out, he justifies in terms of man's fall from grace, is a kind of compromise between suicide and Father D'Arcy, "a Jesuit philosopher who had the monopoly for converting the English intellectuals." But Miss Spark's universe is Kierkegaardian rather than Hegelian; Nick must choose.

Choose he does when, after first unsuccessfully trying to draw attention to the stabbing he has witnessed, he finds himself next to the knife-wielding seaman and simply slips a letter into his pocket. The letter is a forgery by Jane Wright (who makes extra money by eliciting holograph responses from famous writers with phony letters), purporting to be a critic's praise of the *Notebooks* as a work of genius. Giving away the letter, Nick repudiates a way of life; he rejects a clever and aphoristic, and therefore distorted and oversimplified, interpretation of reality. And since the letter is false, he is also rejecting moral duplicity, hypocritical posing, superficial values. In doing no more than passing the letter on, he recognizes his lack of the right to judge.

Related to this is the Schiaparelli dress, for which Selina is willing to rush back into a burning building, and which, of more concern to her than the lives of her friends, is clearly symbolic of the superficial, the showy, the glittering façade that often covers a moral void. Examples of hypocrisy and shallowness pervade the book: Colonel Dobrell's wife, member of the Ethical Guardians, who censor hometown literature in America; Jane's false letters; Pauline Fox's fictitious dates with the famous Jack Buchanan; Selina's legendary poise. It is, in fact, Selina's "poise" in the catastrophe that provides the novel's climactic nightmare. Her complete disregard for human values—the "savage action"—is morally a profounder violation of human dignity than the seaman's act, and is consigned to a lower circle of Miss Spark's Hell.

All, even the Schiaparelli dress, survive the fire, except Joanna Childe. A teacher of elocution, she recites poetry throughout the book, and, a rector's daughter, she dies singing a hymn. "She had a sense of Hell," Nicholas tells her shallow father, whom Miss Spark describes as a shepherd of the "best prime mutton." And in her devotion to poetry she has a sense of beauty that goes beyond the glittering dress or Selina's poise. However, not only does Joanna die, her recitation of "The Wreck of the Deutschland," a poem relevant to her death, is erased from its tape for reasons of postwar economy. In short, Joanna Childe, whose name suggests innocence, and all traces of her, are completely eradicated, while Selina and the dress survive; the murderous sailor slips away into the crowd, while Nicholas is martyred physically in Haiti and spiritually by his former acquaintances in England. As in Hopkins' great poem, there is no humanly understandable ethical system implicit in catastrophe; man's relation to God cannot be systematized, but must be experienced by the individual who transcends all attempts to rationalize divinity. And as in "Adonais" and "Ode to the West Wind," poems frequently recited by Joanna, there is for the poet-prophet—and perhaps Nicholas is one—a way of transcending the limits of the human condition. As far the guilty, the sailor, Selina, and those who are simply shallow, their punishment lies precisely in the meanness of their lives. But however rationalized, the vision of this novel is, like Hopkins', terrible.

In 1965 Miss Spark published the most complex, most ambitious of her novels. As its title indicates, *The Mandelbaum Gate* takes place in divided Jerusalem. However, like the island in *Robinson*, this city is a place of the mind as well as a geographical reality; split in two, it becomes an emblem of all "split" characters, of whom there are an abundance in the novel. Most obvious, and most important, is Barbara Vaughan, the "Gentile Jewess," who struggles toward religious and moral identity. Then there are Freddy Hamilton, whose more daring qualities emerge for a brief period and overrule his staid façade, and Miss Rickward (Ricky), man-hating schoolmistress, Barbara's friend and boss, who tumbles passionately into bed with her guide while searching for Barbara. And the list could be extended to include all important characters, ending with Adolf Eichmann, whose trial is in progress throughout the novel, and whose bureaucratic mediocrity and monstrous actions seem totally incompatible.

What each of these characters has in common is a rational, calm surface, which is sometimes in conflict with an irrational, passionate inner self. And, to return to the macrocosm, the city of Jerusalem itself is split in precisely this way. There is on the one hand rational, scientific Israel—Barbara begins by chaffing the Israeli guides who show her industrial progress at the expense of Christian religious sites, and ends wanting "to run along the pavements of the sweet, rational streets"—and on the other the bizarre, devious, emotional Arab world.

The Jordanian side of the boundary, where the inhibitions of Barbara Vaughan, Freddy Hamilton, and Ricky are broken down, seems to correspond to the prelogical, desire-controlled Id, and pragmatic, sensible Israel to the Ego. The functions of the Superego, originally the voice of the parents and society but eventually an integral part of the psyche, are appropriately embodied in the former "protectors" of Palestine, the British, who are no longer officially in charge, but who exert a definite moral influence (at least on the Ego; they are notoriously less effective in Arab territory).

The lessons of *Robinson* are repeated, but their implications are broader. Once again, it is essential to confront the dark centers of the self, the irrational, in order to be able to function consciously and rationally. And once again the unconscious is a morally ambivalent source of energy. For Barbara, Freddy, and Ricky, its temporary dominance means an end to much repression and the beginning of true insight into the self, the effects of which remain even after the return to the rational world. But this plunge to the depths is always dangerous, and holds at least the possibility of self-destruction (here symbolically at the hands of the Arabs, frantically alert for Israeli spies); and the irrational is also a possible danger for others, so much so that the reasonable parts of the psyche have the responsibility to investigate and punish any impingement of the darker side, a responsibility fulfilled by the Israelis in the Eichmann trial.

Where *The Mandelbaum Gate* differs from *Robinson*—and it is a difference crucial to artistic success as well as profundity of insight—is in the degree of dependence of the novel upon its allegorical framework. While the most significant action in the earlier book is allegorical, allegory in *The Mandelbaum Gate* reinforces, but does not replace or overshadow, the examination of individual characters. Muriel Spark, obsessed here by the apparent fundamental split in the nature of all being, sees this split everywhere, and concentrates on its psychological and moral instances.

As the city of Jerusalem centers on the Mandelbaum Gate, so Miss Spark's novel centers on Barbara Vaughan. Her mother Jewish, her father gentile, she herself finally a Catholic convert, Barbara is thirty-seven years old and a spinster when she meets archeologist Harry Clegg. Their passionate affair apparently cannot end in marriage because Harry has been previously married and divorced, and is therefore, in the eyes of the Church, married. Previously able to confront experience and to unite the disparate sides of her nature—Jewishness and sexuality, Christianity and spirituality, have always been associated in her mind—she now finds her values not simply threatened but inapplicable, "inadequate to cope with the whole of her experience."

When Harry goes to Palestine to work, Barbara, who had broken off the sexual part of their affair as a result of her conflict, goes on a pilgrimage to the Holy Land, beginning in Israel and planning ultimately to cross into Jordan. Harry has petitioned Rome, with little hope, for an annulment of his first marriage, but Barbara, first considering giving Harry up, finally decides she will marry him no matter what the Vatican's decision.

The situation is complicated by Barbara's Jewishness, which, symbolic of sexual drives, provoked the crisis to begin with (the book's symbolism is complicated here by the fact that Jewishness seems to stand in the same relation to Christianity as the Arab world does to Israel); appropriately, it is this hidden aspect of her identity that places her in danger of being killed by the Arabs if they find her out. This becomes likely when her coming pilgrimage gets into the papers, and only Freddy Hamilton's sudden change in character makes possible the intricate, sometimes clumsy and bungling, plans that ultimately save her.

There are further complications, principally the birth certificate forged by Ricky, indicating that Harry Clegg, whose origins are obscure, was born a Catholic. She has changed his religion to "save" Barbara from marriage, but ironically it is precisely this document that makes the marriage possible. (If Harry was not a Catholic, the Church would recognize the marriage but not the divorce; however, if he was a Catholic and married outside the Church, the marriage itself would be invalid.) But these machinations are not simply anticlimactic; they are quite beside the point. Barbara has already decided to marry Clegg, and it is on this decision that we must focus, for it represents the elimination of Barbara's "split," the resolution of her conflict:

"Either the whole of life is unified under God or everything falls apart. Sex is child's play in the argument." She was thinking of the Eichmann trial, and was aware that there were other events too, which rolled away the stone that revealed an empty hole in the earth, that led to a bottomless pit.

From limited sensibility, unable to encompass important aspects of her experience, Barbara approaches the unity of being frequently sought but rarely found in Miss Spark's novels. In Eichmann, and in her own darker nature, she sees a void beyond conventional moralities, a void that forces man to encounter experience without props, to realize there is no code that relieves him of the burdens of choice. And the empty pit is not simply the heart of darkness within man, although it certainly is that, but also the emptiness of death, the meaninglessness life threatens to have unless we give it form. As Muriel Spark has repeatedly made perfectly clear, being a Catholic does not simplify giving form to one's life; it may even be a handicap.

Freddy Hamilton, not as consciously aware as Barbara of the need to find his true self, finds his unconscious doing it for him. For several days, the memory of which comes back slowly and only after long probing, Freddy breaks the habitual mold of his life. A middle-aged Englishman in the foreign service, with an unhappy marriage buried well in the past, he is the model of superficial decency and decorum. As far from home as he has been most of his life, his ties with his mother are strong—he receives a continuous stream of letters from her, mostly concerned with the tension between herself and long-time servant "Benny," and the need for Freddy to do something about it.

It is Barbara, intent on going on her pilgrimage in spite of all obstacles, who by actions and words shakes Freddy's world. When Freddy, "afraid she had some tiresome deep conviction," responds to Barbara's dilemma with platitudes, she quotes Apocalypse: "I know of thy doings, and find thee neither cold nor hot; cold or hot, I would thou were one or the other. Being what thou art, lukewarm, neither cold nor hot, thou wilt make me vomit thee out of my mouth." At first taken aback, Freddy is profoundly influenced. When he and Barbara are at the Cartwrights (Freddy's friends) at the start of her Jordanian trip, he reacts to their lack of commitment by quoting the same passage. And this is later his last memory before the lost days.

What happens during the blank period is that Freddy blows both cold and hot: he tears up letters to and about his mother and flushes them down the toilet; he engineers, with a friend, the plot to spirit Barbara from her convent lodging to her secret pilgrimage (a symbolic act for both parties); and he has a one-night affair with his friend's mistress. This is such powerful stuff for Freddy that he loses memory of it, as well as of his discovery that a colleague and his wife are spies. But it all comes back to him later, amazing him with awareness of his full possibilities, of the limitations of his customary existence. Freedom, however, as Freddy learns, brings responsibility and guilt. His failure to mail the letters leads—at least in his own mind—to Benny's murdering his mother; facing the abyss has its destructive elements.

Technically the most complex of Miss Spark's novels, *The*

Mandelbaum Gate explores a world whose texture is equally involved. Miss Spark writes of Freddy regaining his memory: "The details followed gradually, throughout the days and into the years ahead and they occurred, then, in those fragments, more or less distorted, which are the normal formations and decor of human memory." The novel proceeds in very much the same way. Fragments are revealed, with a continuous movement back and forth in time. The comparatively simple structure of *Slender Means* and *Jean Brodie*, that is, the fairly regular alternation of two sequences of narrative, is here complicated by the stream of association of each character moving the action unpredictably in time. In addition, multiplicity of perspective suggests a world defined by individual human perception rather than one describable in terms of an absolute system.

The critical response to *The Mandelbaum Gate* was relatively cool, and in her latest novel, *The Public Image*, Miss Spark has returned to less complex forms. More or less conventionally narrated, the new book, with its diminished cast of characters, centers almost exclusively on its heroine. Not especially striking in appearance or talent, Annabel Christopher owes her success as a movie star to her image, developed on screen by her director, off screen by public relations work. To the world, she appears to possess an elegant, controlled exterior covering a smoldering furnace within. There is, however, nothing within but a vague emptiness overlaid with secondhand responses to experience. Her husband, Frederick, is engulfed by the role he must play in his wife's public image, and, after a futile struggle to maintain an image of his own, kills himself in a way calculated to destroy his wife's façade. Annabel, only imperfectly successful in evading his trap, is left with an awareness of her inner void, and, in her feelings for her child, at least the possibility of developing a real self. Her last action is to leave Rome for Greece; that is, symbolically to search out the origins of the Romans' adopted culture.

Many of Miss Spark's hallmarks are present: the interplay between illusion and reality (here reinforced by the symbolism of the cinema); a blackmailer (critic Billy O'Brien); a set of deceitful letters (Frederick's); a symbolic landscape (Rome). But more than in previous novels, Miss Spark has difficulty infusing life into her ever present sense of the grotesque. The decision to place Annabel, in all her shallowness, near the center of consciousness proves a formidable obstacle. Banality always threatens; even a character as potentially dynamic as Frederick is lost in the shadow of Annabel's dullness.

Muriel Spark's achievement to this point is more than respectable. Unified by recurring motifs and configurations, her apparently glib novels comprise a serious attempt to probe the dark moral heart of man. Although often in danger of over-emphasizing the intellectual structure of her writing—the ever-present suggestion of allegory, the series of contrived parallels and symmetrical arrangements of character and incident, the dominant obsessions to which most of her books can be reduced—Muriel Spark, at her best, reaches beyond wit to humanity; then her imaginative extensions of reality, though analyzable, retain something of the irreducible wholeness of experience.

SELECTED BIBLIOGRAPHY

NOTE: *A more extensive bibliography of works by and about Muriel Spark has been compiled by Bernard Stone; it appears as an appendix to Derek Stanford's study, listed below. From* The Comforters *to the present, Macmillan has been Miss Spark's English publisher; in America, Lippincott published her work through* The Prime of Miss Jean Brodie, *Knopf since then.*

PRINCIPAL WORKS OF MURIEL SPARK

Tribute to Wordsworth. Edited with Derek Stanford. London, 1950.

Child of Light: A Reassessment of Mary Wollstonecraft Shelley. Hadleigh, Essex, 1951.

A Selection of Poems by Emily Brontë. Editor. London, 1952.

The Fanfarlo and Other Verse. Adlington, Kent, 1952.

My Best Mary: Selected Letters of Mary Shelley. Edited with Derek Stanford. London, 1953.

John Masefield. London, 1953.

Emily Brontë: Her Life and Work. With Derek Stanford. London, 1953.

The Brontë Letters. Editor. London, 1954.

Letters of John Henry Newman. Edited with Derek Stanford. London, 1957.

The Comforters. London, 1957. Philadelphia and New York, 1958.

Robinson. London, 1958. Philadelphia and New York, 1958.

The Go-Away Bird and Other Stories. London, 1958. Philadelphia and New York, 1960.

Memento Mori. London, 1959. Philadelphia and New York, 1959.

The Ballad of Peckham Rye. London, 1960. Philadelphia and New York, 1960.

The Bachelors. London, 1960. Philadelphia and New York, 1961.

Voices at Play: Stories and Ear-Pieces. London, 1961. Philadelphia and New York, 1962.

The Prime of Miss Jean Brodie. London, 1961. Philadelphia and New York, 1962.

"My Conversion," *Twentieth Century*, CLXX (Autumn, 1961), 58–63.

"Edinburgh-born," *New Statesman*, LXIV (August 10, 1962), 180.

Doctors of Philosophy. A Play. London, 1963.

The Girls of Slender Means. London, 1963. New York, 1963.

The Mandelbaum Gate. London, 1965. New York, 1965.

Collected Stories I. London, 1967. New York, 1968.

Collected Poems I. London, 1967. New York, 1968.

The Public Image. London, 1968.

CRITICAL WORKS AND COMMENTARY

Adler, Renata. "Muriel Spark," in On Contemporary Literature. Edited by Richard Kostelanetz. New York, 1964. Pp. 591–96.

Baldanza, Frank. "Muriel Spark and the Occult," Wisconsin Studies in Contemporary Literature, VI (Summer, 1965), 190–203.

Hoyt, Charles Alva. "Muriel Spark: The Surrealist Jane Austen," in Contemporary British Novelists. Edited by Charles Shapiro. Carbondale and Edwardsville, Ill., 1965. Pp. 125–43.

Kermode, Frank. "House of Fiction" (includes interview with Miss Spark), Partisan Review, XXX (Spring, 1963), 61–82.

——— "The Novel as Jerusalem," Atlantic Monthly, CCXVI (October, 1965), 92–98.

——— "The Prime of Miss Muriel Spark," New Statesman, LXVI (September 27, 1963), 397–98.

Murphy, Carol. "A Spark of the Supernatural," Approach, No. 60 (Summer, 1966), pp. 26–30.

Ohmann, Carol. "Muriel Spark's Robinson," Critique: Studies in Modern Fiction, VIII (Fall, 1965), 70–84.

Potter, Nancy. "Muriel Spark: Transformer of the Commonplace," Renascence, XVII (Spring, 1965), 115–20.

Raven, Simon. "Heavens Below," Spectator, No. 7056 (September 20, 1963), p. 354.

Schneider, Harold. "A Writer in Her Prime: The Fiction of Muriel Spark," Critique: Studies in Modern Fiction, V (Fall, 1962), 28–45.

Stanford, Derek. Muriel Spark: A Biographical and Critical Study. With a bibliography by Bernard Stone. Fontwell, Sussex, 1963.

Updike, John. "Creatures of Air," New Yorker, XXXVII (September 30, 1961), 161–67.

Wildman, John Hazard. "Translated by Muriel Spark," in Nine Essays in Modern Literature. Edited by Donald Stanford. Baton Rouge, 1965. Pp. 129–44.